PUBLISHED BY
DARE WRIGHT MEDIA, LLC

WWW.DAREWRIGHT.COM

**MMXX**

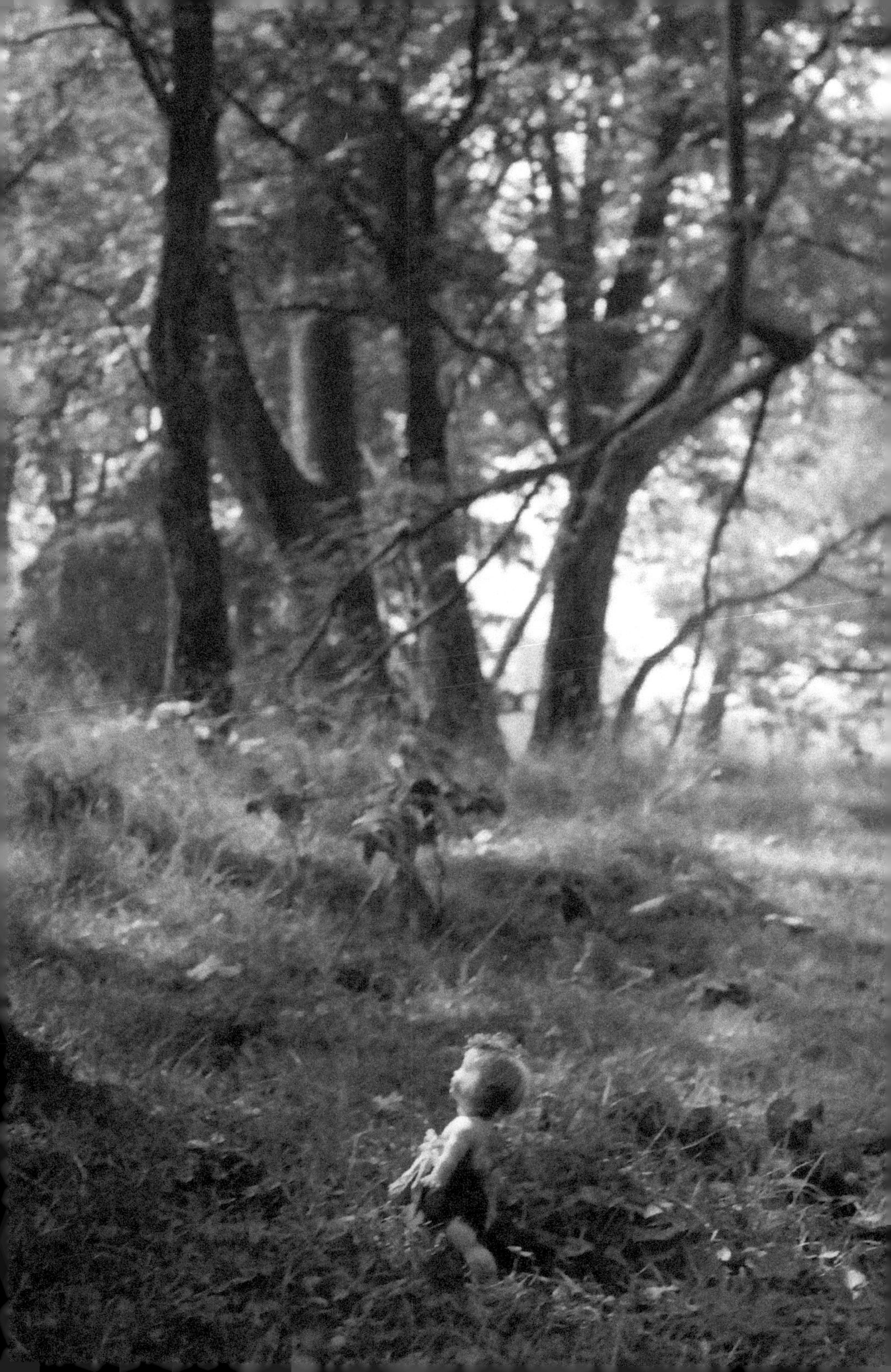

FOR MY GODDAUGHTER
SUSAN SANDEMAN

WRIGHT, DARE.
TAKE ME HOME / STORY AND PHOTOGRAPHS
BY DARE WRIGHT – HARDBACK EDITION.
50 PAGES
SUMMARY: A LITTLE DOLL NAMED ROBIN LIVES HAPPILY AMONG THE WILD ANIMALS IN A FOREST UNTIL SHE'S DISCOVERED BY A YOUNG GIRL NAMED SUSAN WHO TAKES THE DOLL HOME WITH HER. ALTHOUGH ROBIN QUICKLY FINDS NEW FRIENDS AMONG SUSAN'S OTHER TOYS, SHE MISSES HER REAL HOME AND FRIENDS IN THE WOODS TERRIBLY. WHEN HER FRIEND CROW EVENTUALLY FINDS ROBIN, HE HELPS HER RETURN TO HER HOME IN THE WILD.
AUDIENCE: AGES 4-10.

ISBN: 978-1-7334312-2-4

Copyright © 1965 by Dare Wright; © 2020 by Dare Wright Media, LLC. All Rights Reserved.

No part of this book may be reproduced, stored in a retrieval system, or transmitted in any form or by any means – electronic, mechanical, recording, or otherwise – without the prior written consent of the publisher, excepting brief quotes used in connection with print and online reviews.

The Lonely Doll® is a registered trademark of Dare Wright Media, LLC.

email: info@darewright.com

Hardback Edition Published by Dare Wright Media, LLC in 2020.

# TAKE ME HOME

STORY AND PHOTOGRAPHS BY
**DARE WRIGHT**
Author Of The Lonely Doll Series

Most dolls belong to little girls, and live in houses. Robin was different.

Robin was a little doll who lived in the woods.

She didn't belong to anyone, but she had more friends than she could count.

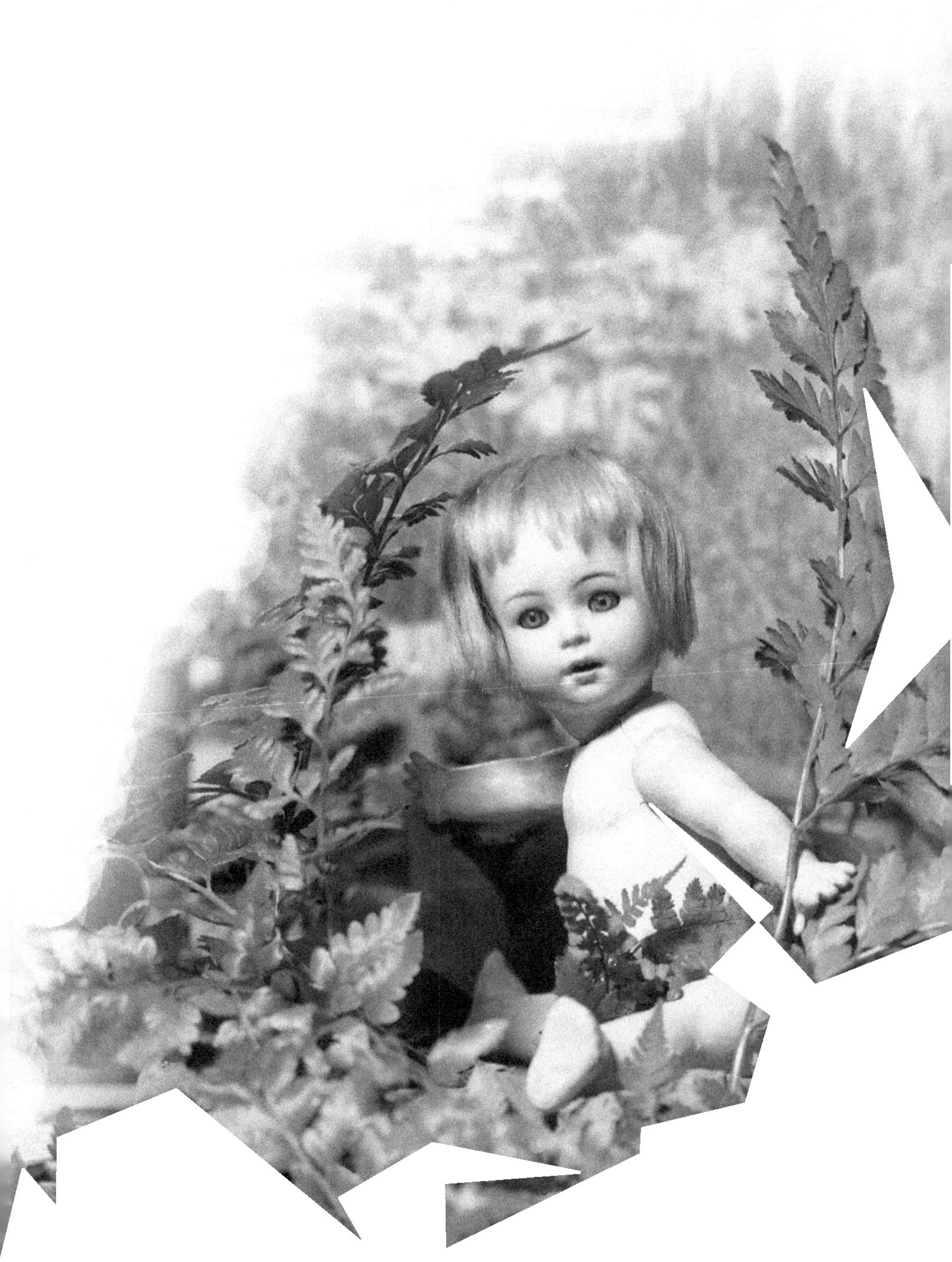

The small wild creatures all loved Robin, and she loved every squirrel and rabbit and bird in the woods.

Even grumpy old Crow, who was always scolding Robin, really loved her very much indeed.

Robin wore dresses made of leaves, or none at all. She bathed in brooks, and lived on honey, berries, and sunshine.

She was happy from morning to night.

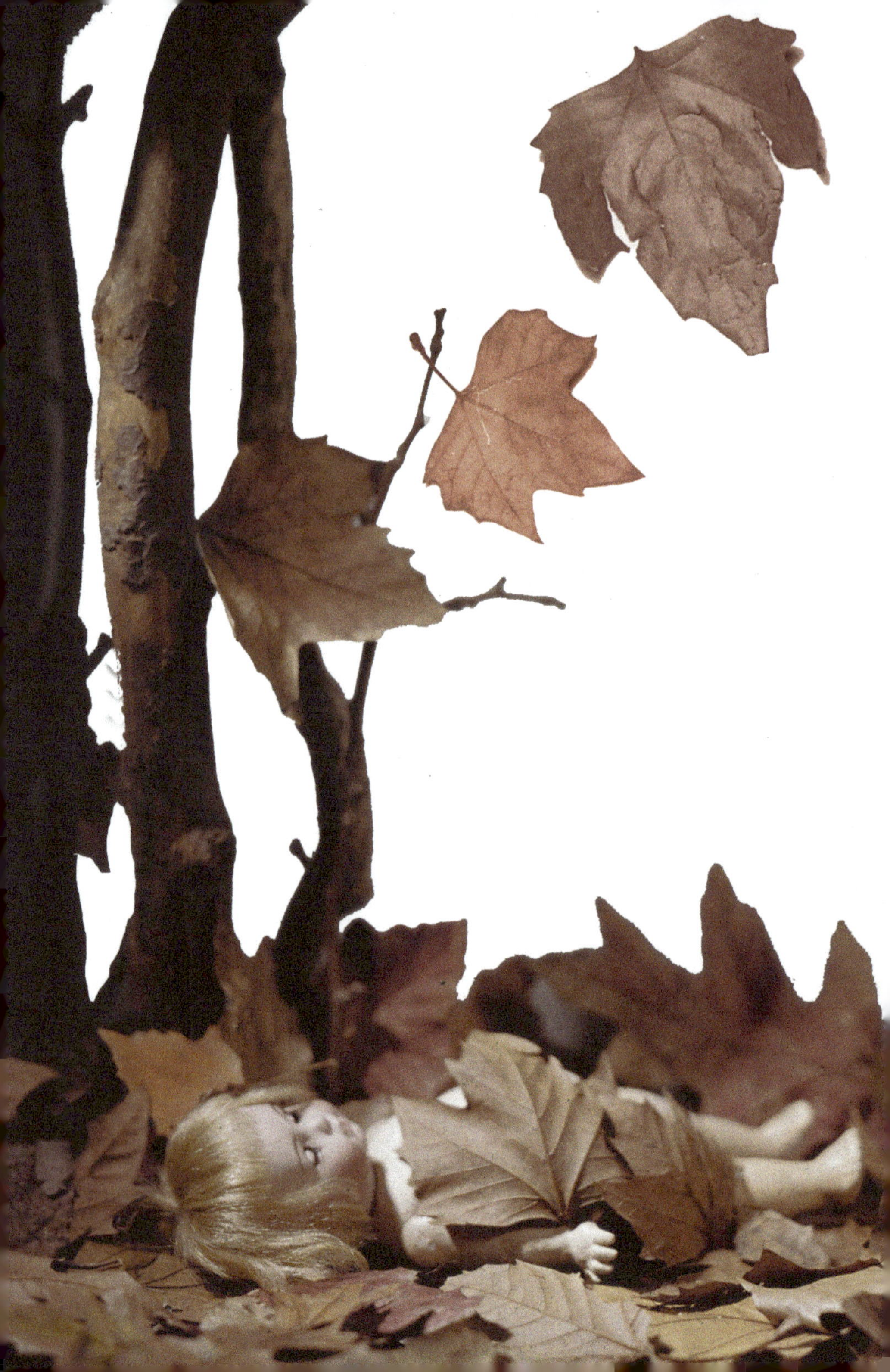

Summer's green days were over, and the cold winds of autumn were blowing when a little girl named Susan came walking through Robin's wood.

Susan saw a doll lying among the leaves.

It was Robin taking an afternoon nap, but Susan thought it was a poor little doll whom nobody wanted.

So Susan picked Robin up, and carried her away.

"Put me down, put me down," Robin kept shouting. "I live in the woods. It's my home."

But Susan wasn't a little girl who could hear dolls talk.

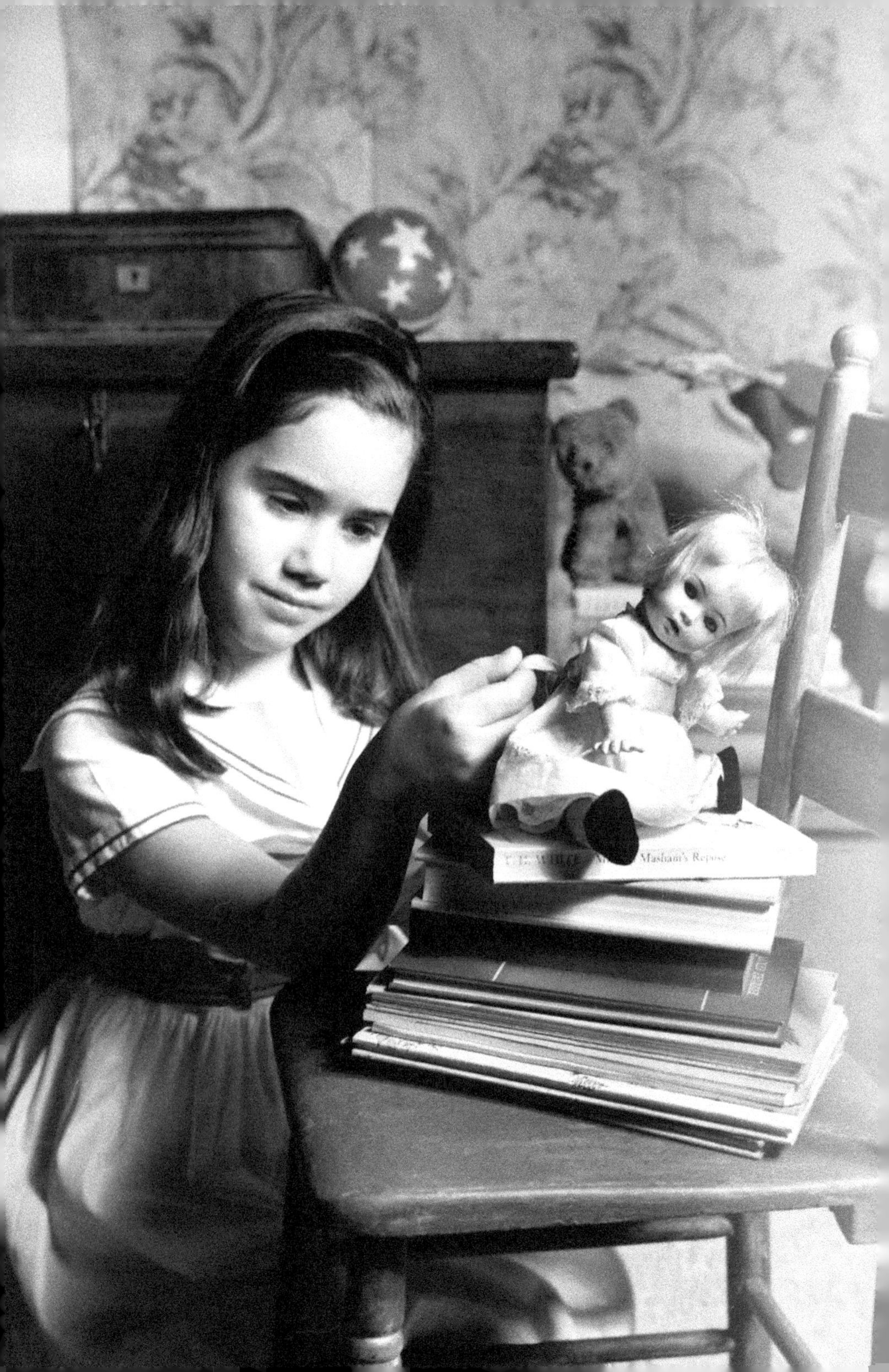
Masham's Repose

She took Robin home with her. She dressed her in a white dress, all starch and frills, and set her down among her toys.

"Hello, everybody," Robin said. "I'm Robin."

"How do you do," said a large doll. "I am Matilda. Welcome to your new home."

"Welcome," echoed the woolly lamb, the red plush reindeer, the pink-eared rabbit, and the small brown bear cub.

"Thank you," said Robin, "but this isn't my home. I live in the woods. Do you know the way back there?"

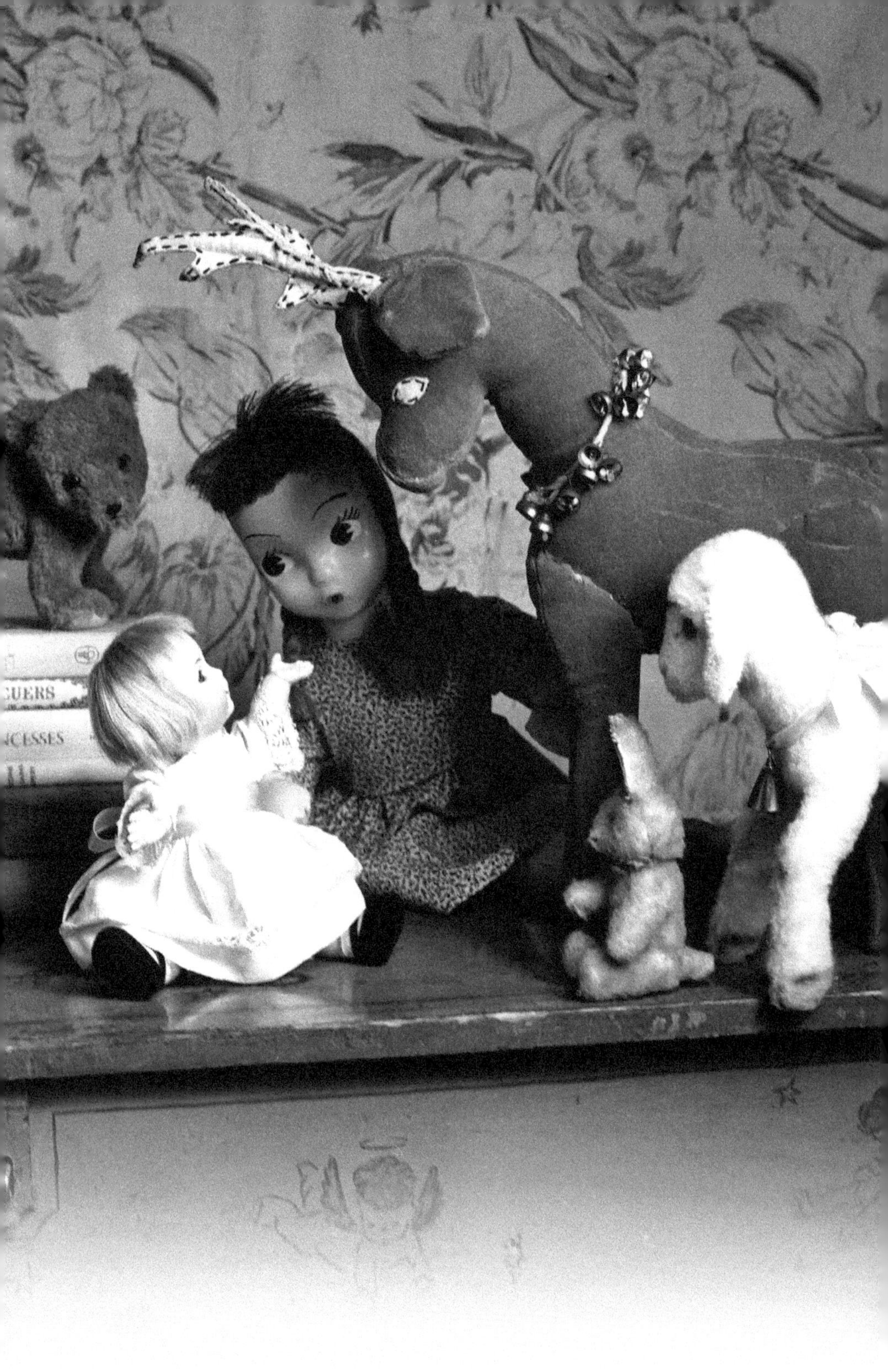

"Nobody lives in the woods except wild animals," said Matilda.

"Well, I do," said Robin. "It's the loveliest place in the world, and the animals are my friends. Just think, woolly lamb, in the woods you could sleep on green grass. Reindeer, you could run through the trees and jump over streams. Little rabbit, you could live with the wild rabbits in their thorny thickets."

"I'd rather sleep on Susan's bed," said the woolly lamb.

"Gracious, I might get my feet wet in the streams," said the deer.

"Thorny thickets!" gasped the rabbit. "They would tear my soft, pink ears. I want to stay with Susan."

"You see how happy we all are here. You will learn to like it too, Robin," said Matilda.

"I won't – not ever!" shouted Robin, and burst into tears.

Then something soft nudged her shoulder, and a gruff little voice said shyly, "I'm Sam, and I'd like to hear more about the woods."

It was the little brown bear cub. Robin flung her arms around his neck, and began to talk. She talked and talked until Sam knew all about how lovely it was to live in the woods.

"Please," begged Sam when Robin paused for breath, "will you take me home with you when you go? I know that bears live in the woods, and I'm a bear. Please, Robin."

"Of course I will. I promise, cross my heart," said Robin.

"How will you get out of the house? You are very small," said Sam.

"I'm big enough," said Robin. "I'll find a way."

And she went off to sleep with her head against Sam's soft side.

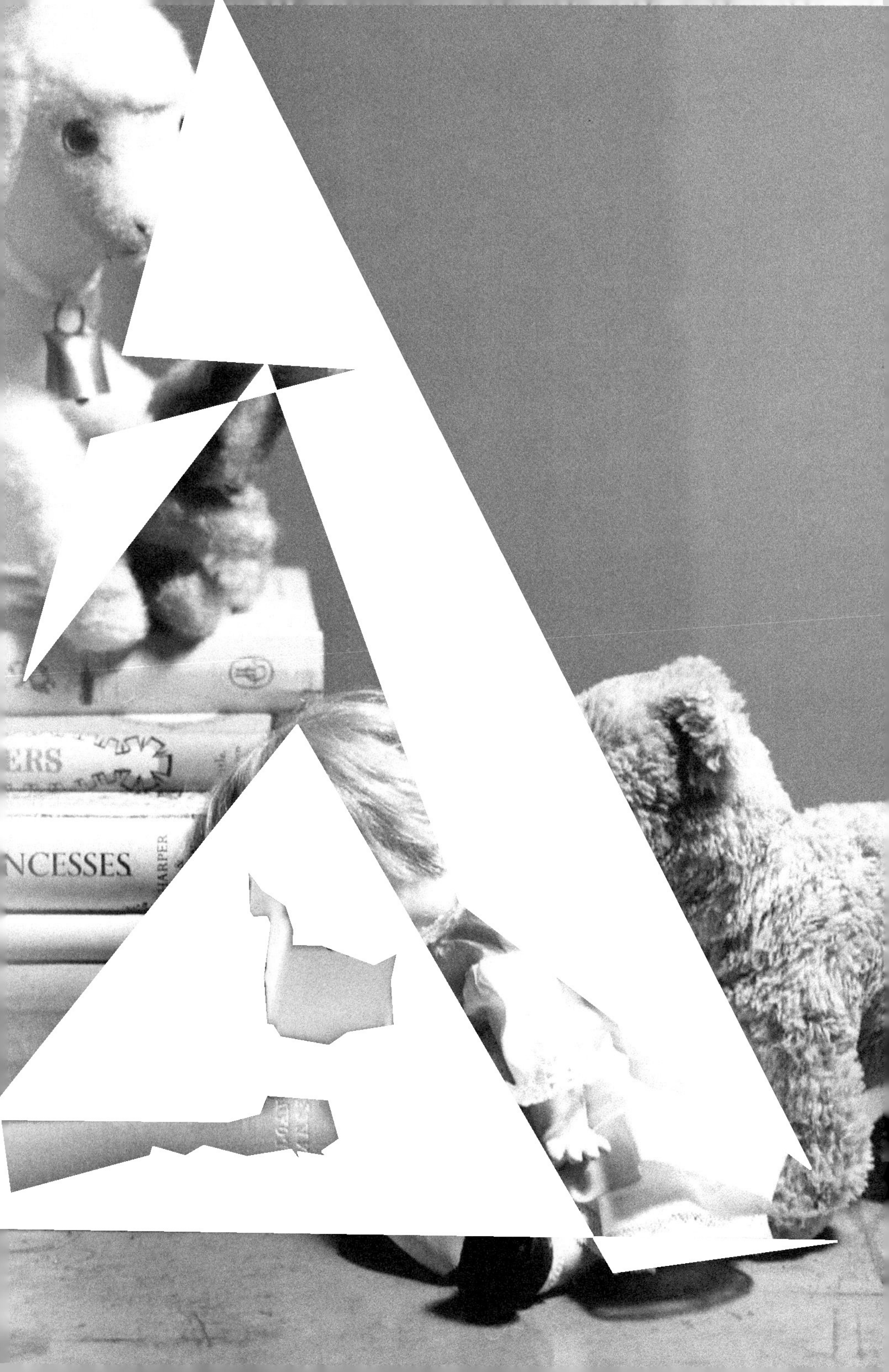
ERS
NCESSES
HARPER

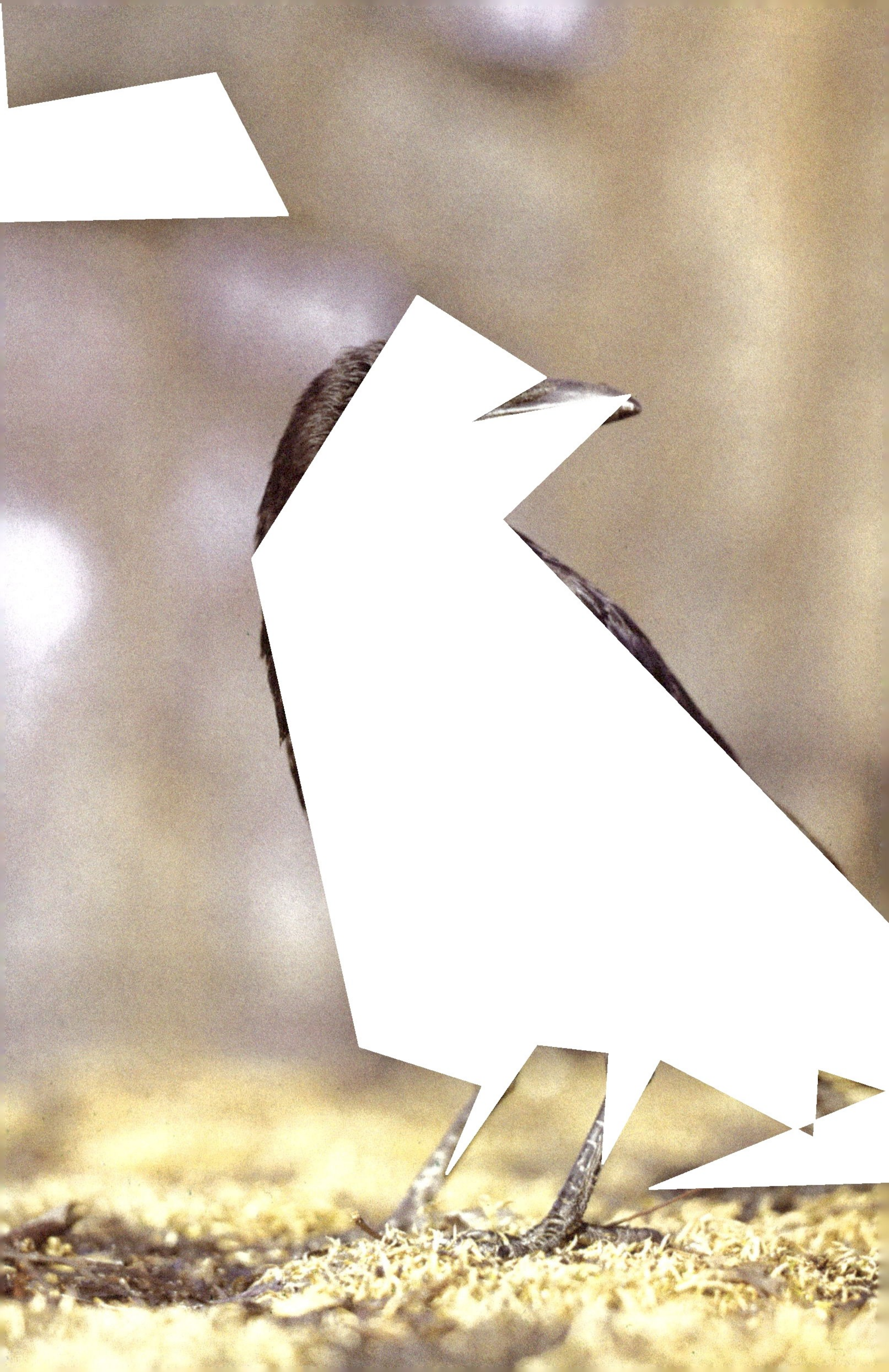

All through the woods the whisper was running, "Where's Robin? Robin is gone. Where's Robin?"

"I saw a little girl on the path through the woods this afternoon," said a squirrel.

"I saw Robin asleep right beside the path," said a rabbit.

"That little girl has kidnapped our Robin," they all cried together. "Where's Crow? He'll know what to do."

"Robin kidnapped, you say?" cawed Crow. "Well, don't make such a fuss. I'll soon find her."

Crow flew all about the countryside on his strong wings, peering into window after window.

It was dark when he came to Susan's house. High above the ground was an open, lighted window. Inside, Crow saw Robin sound asleep with Sam watching over her.

One caw from Crow woke Robin, and she nearly choked him with hugs and kisses.

"Stop mussing my feathers," said Crow. "What ever's the matter?"

"Oh, Crow, take me home," cried Robin. "I don't like being indoors, and wearing a dress. Everybody but Sam makes fun of living in the woods. This is my friend Sam. He's coming home with me. He understands me, but that little girl doesn't even hear me when I talk."

"You talk a great deal too much," said Crow, "and you make friends too fast. Take that bear home? No!"

"But I promised Sam. You could carry us on your back," said Robin.

"I could not!" croaked Crow. "I might ruin my fine wings."

"Sam and I aren't very big."

"No," said Crow. "I'll find a way out for you but not for that bear."

"He's my friend," said Robin.

"He's not my friend," said Crow. "Come without him, or stay here."

"I'll have to stay," sighed Robin.

Crow flew off in a temper. He knew that he was behaving badly and that made him even crosser.

The woods were very quiet without the small doll. There was no little voice chattering all day, no yellow head bobbing among the leaves.

"I like it this way. It's peaceful. She always did talk too much," said Crow.

"We miss her," said all the birds and animals. "Bring her home."

"What difference will one little bear make?" said a turtle. "We might like him. Let him come, Crow."

"I don't want him," said Crow. "If Robin prefers that bear to us, let her stay where she is. I don't miss her."

But just the same, Crow was always flying over to Susan's to find out if Robin had changed her mind.

"Sam's my friend, and I'll never, never go without him," declared Robin, although she grew more homesick every day.

Robin wouldn't budge, and neither would Crow.

"Go without me," said Sam. "I didn't mean to cause all this trouble. Tell Crow you'll go."

"Never," said Robin, and she hugged him.

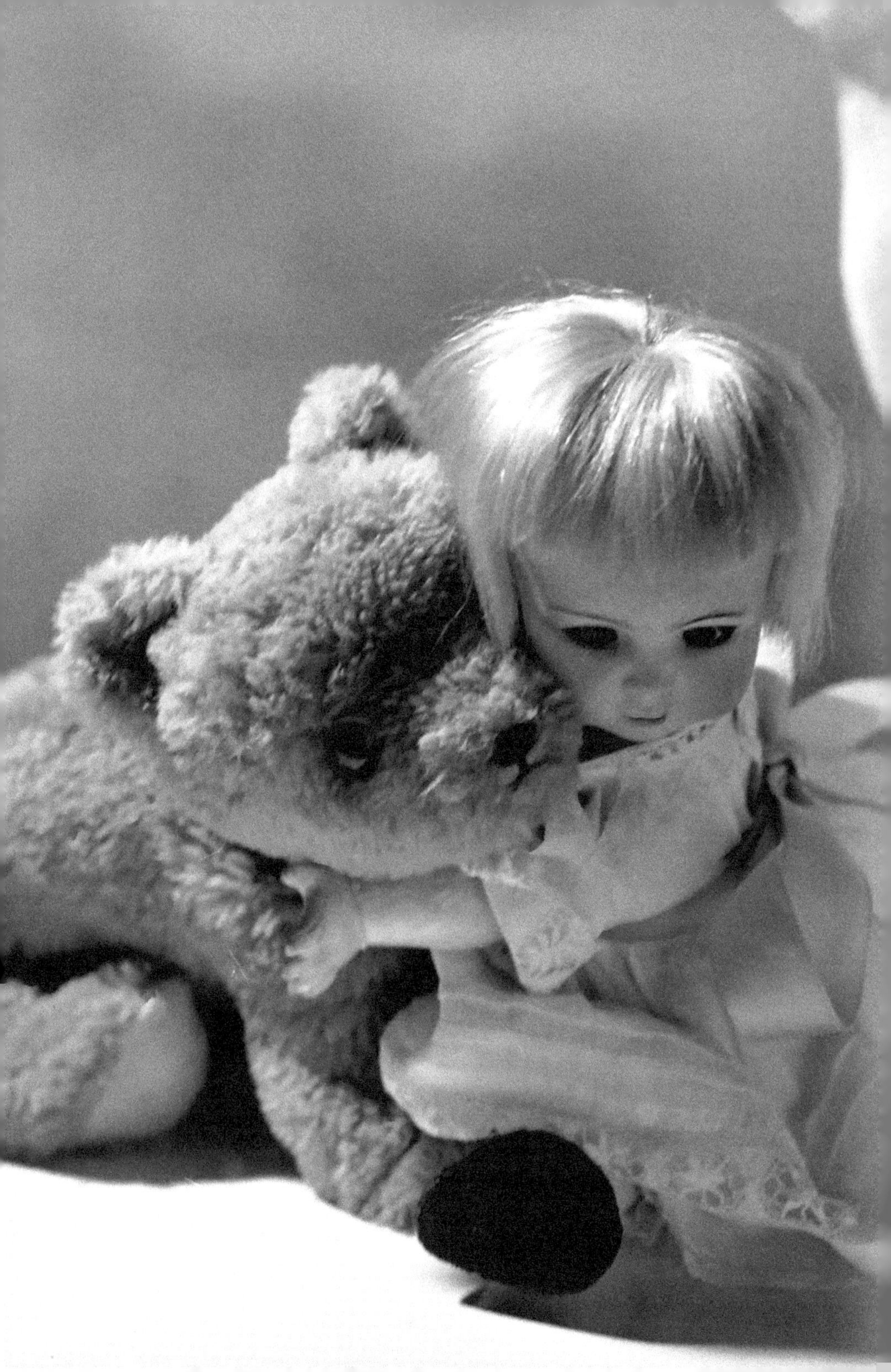

The days grew longer, and darker, and colder. The first snow fell.

Susan's parents decided it was time to move back to the city.

When Crow heard this news he said, "Good! They'll take that interfering little bear along with them, and you'll come home where you belong, Robin."

"No, I'll have to stay with Sam, and they'll take me to the city too," cried Robin.

"Take you! They'll do no such thing!" croaked Crow in alarm.

"They will if I'm here. Oh, Crow, please rescue Sam and me before it's too late," begged Robin.

Crow thought of Robin gone from the woods forever. He gave in.

"All right, all right!" he cawed. "Be ready tonight."

"Sam too?" asked Robin.

"Sam too," said Crow, "but you'll be sorry. He'll be a nuisance."

As soon as darkness came Robin and Sam started waiting on the cold window sill.

The snow-covered ground lay far below them.

How could Crow ever get them away?

The moon rose, and, with a swish of black wings, Crow landed beside them.

"Turn on the light," he ordered, "and get that big black umbrella that stands in the corner. We're going to use it for a parachute."

"Oh, Crow, how clever you are!" cried Robin.

"Of course," said Crow, preening his feathers.

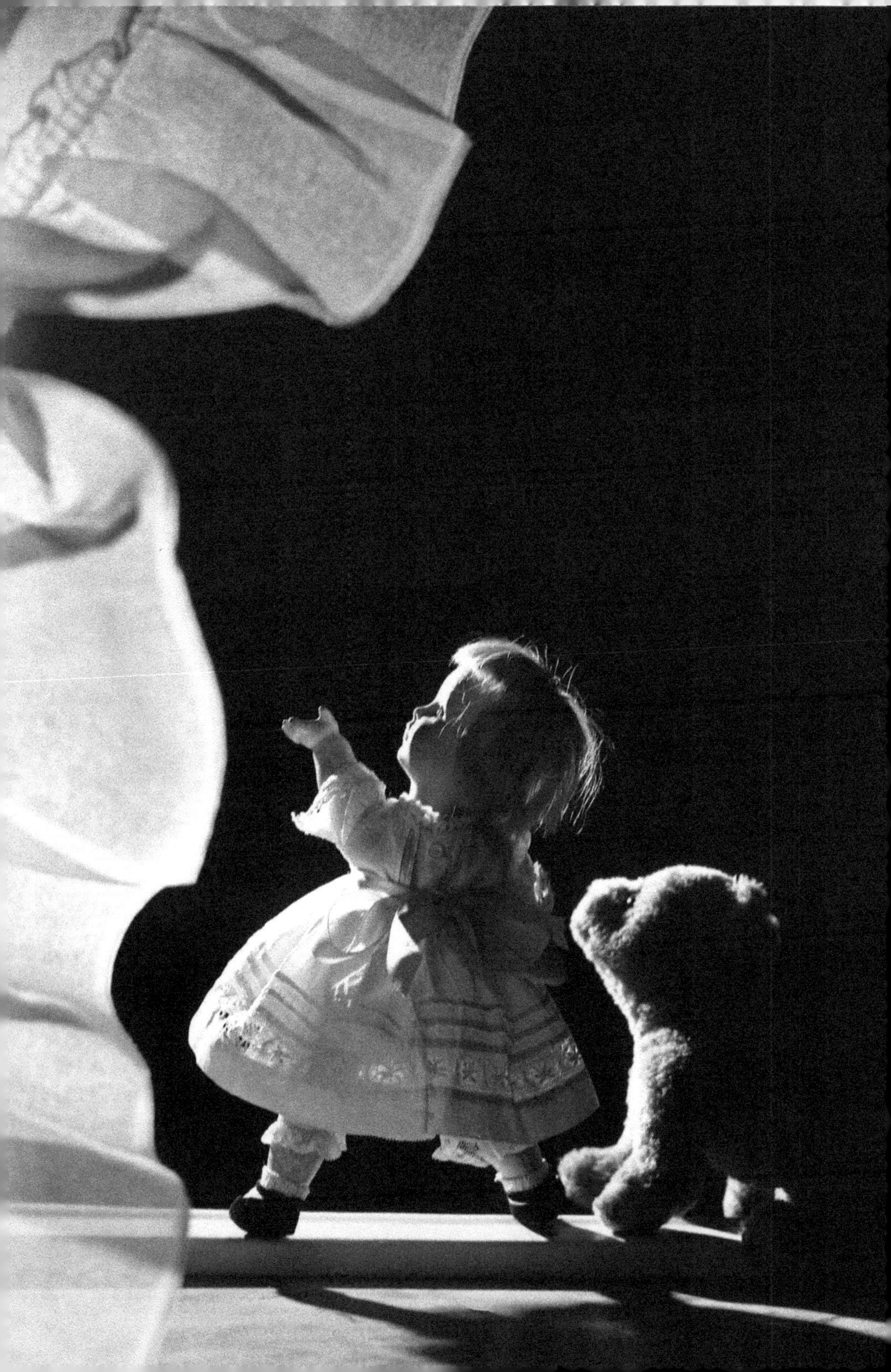

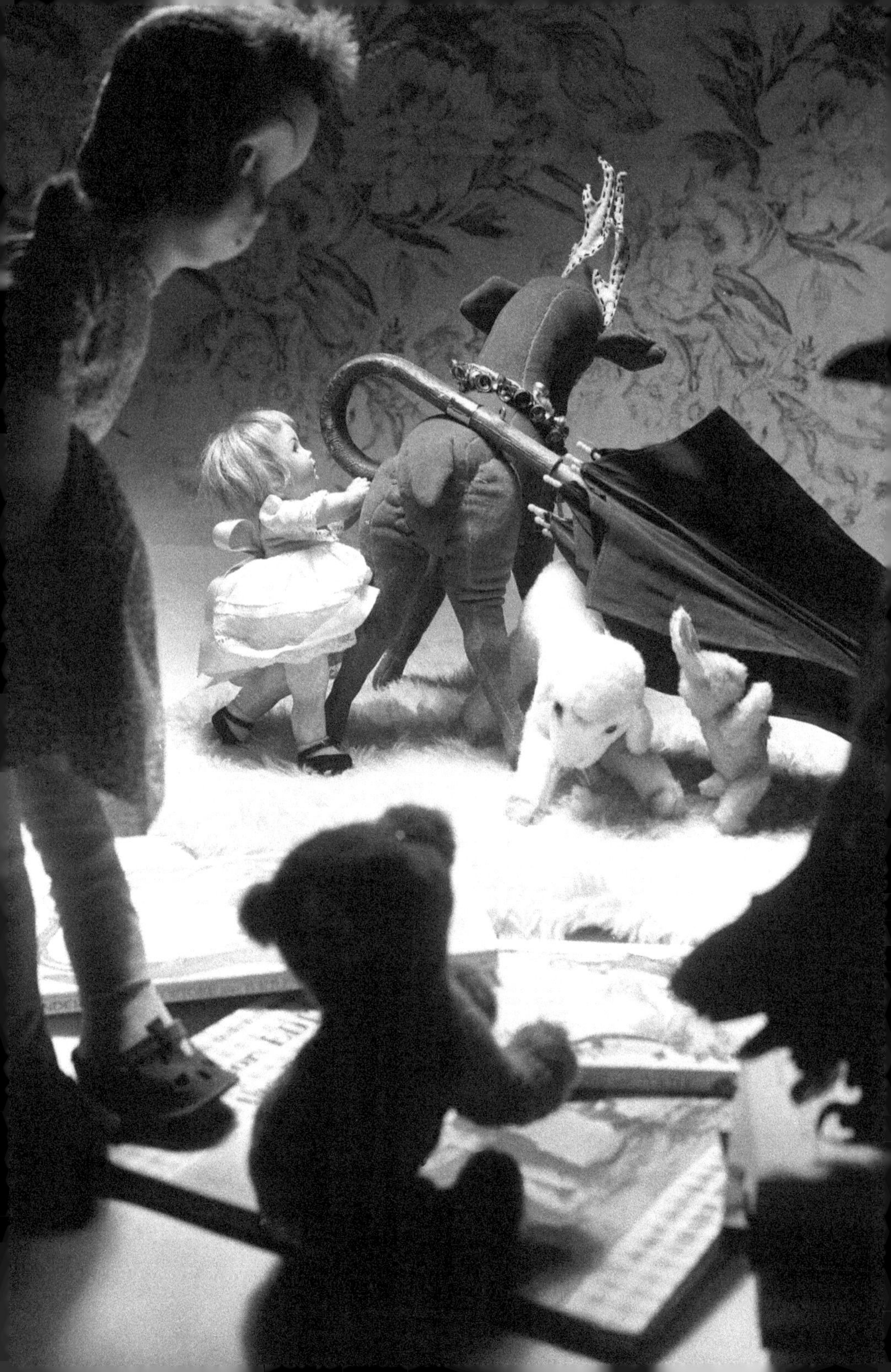

All the toys helped except Matilda who stood and sniffed.

"Very unsafe – these parachutes," she said. "It'll never work."

"It will too, and Sam and I aren't afraid," said Robin.

"You and Sam are quite mad. Imagine leaving a good home with a nice child to live in some dreadful woods. So uncivilized." Matilda shuddered. "And what will Susan think when she finds you gone? After all, she's been very kind to you."

"I suppose she meant to be kind," said Robin. "I'll leave her a letter. And I'm not going home to the woods in this frilly dress. All my friends would laugh at me. Why, I couldn't even climb a tree in it. Unbutton me, please, Matilda," said Robin.

"It's a lovely dress, you ungrateful little thing," said Matilda. "Just what do you expect to wear in the woods?"

"Well, usually I wear leaves," said Robin.

"Leaves! Oh, no!" gasped Matilda. "Leaves! I am shocked, I must say."

"You won't be wearing leaves now," said Crow. "It's winter and the woods are cold. The mice got enough wool from the sheep to make you winter clothes, and I've heard talk of waterproof boots, and beds in hollow trees. Spoiled! That's what you'll be. I told them all so."

"Let's hurry, Crow," said Robin. "I can't wait to get there."

The letter took a long time. Robin didn't write very well, and Crow kept criticizing.

"That's not the way to spell hospitality," he said.

"It's the way I spell it," said Robin.

"Don't be impertinent," said Crow. "Just finish your letter before the whole household is awake."

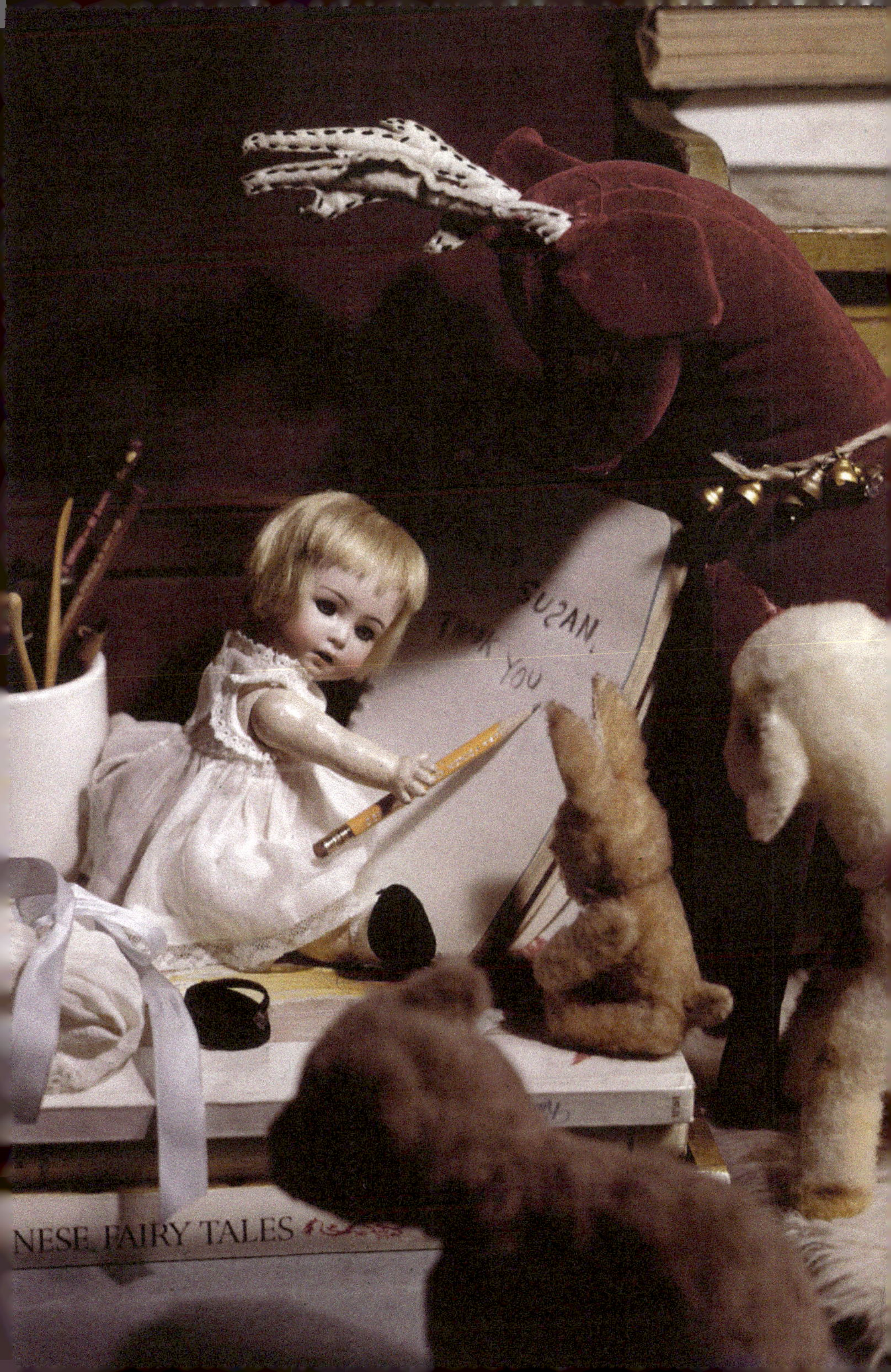
SUSAN,
THANK YOU
NESE FAIRY TALES

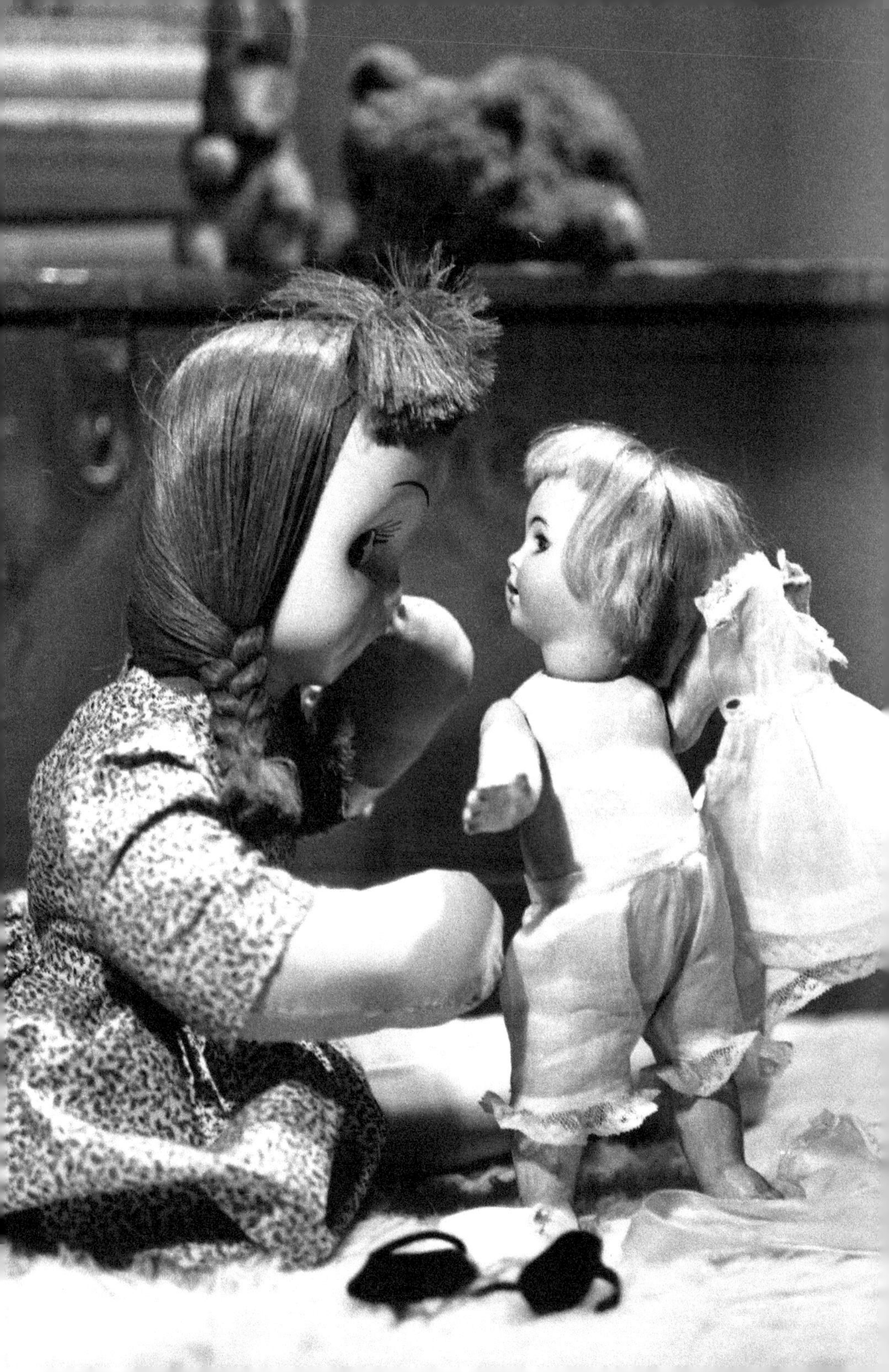

"I'm finished," said Robin, signing her name with a flourish.

"Rather untidy, but I suppose it will do," said Matilda.

The sky was growing light by the time everything was ready.

Robin piled up her white dress, her lace-trimmed petticoat, her blue sash, and her neat shoes and socks. On top she put the letter.

The letter said:

Dear Susan,

Thank you, but I am going away now. I am going back home where I belong. Sam is going with me because bears should live in the woods. Thank you for your horspertality. Good-by.

**ROBIN**

The umbrella was balanced on the window sill.

Robin wedged herself in the crook of the handle.

Sam wrapped his legs around the thin shaft above her.

"Ready?" asked Crow.

With beak and wings he gave a mighty push.

The umbrella wobbled for a moment on the sill.

Robin gasped.

Sam grunted.

What a moment! They were off!

The toys all cheered as Robin and Sam floated gently down.

Sam let go too soon, and landed in a snowdrift.

"I knew he'd be a nuisance," said Crow as he helped dig Sam out.

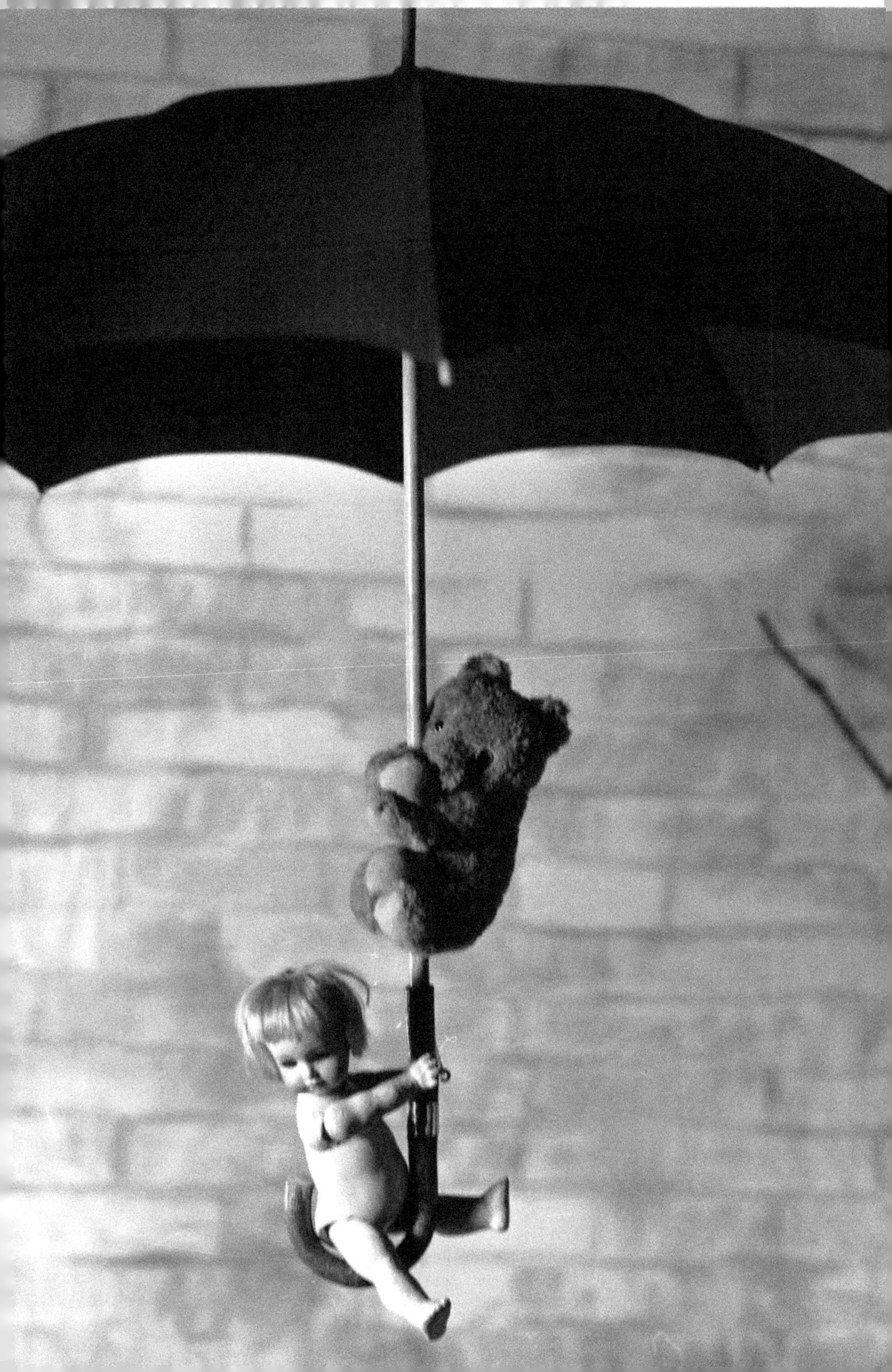

Then off ran Robin and Sam, with Crow flying overhead like a protecting black shadow.

All the winter woods were awake to welcome Robin home.

"We've made you a wool suit. Put it on," squeaked the mice.

"We made you a bed in the hollow tree, and lined it with our softest feathers," chirped the birds.

"We stocked it with our best nuts," chattered the squirrels.

"We've missed you. Welcome back," cried voices from every tree and nest and burrow.

"Thank you, thank you," said Robin. "How lovely to be home! And I've brought my friend Sam with me. You must be nice to him, too...."

Everybody was nice. Even Crow croaked, "perhaps he'll improve, with me to teach him."

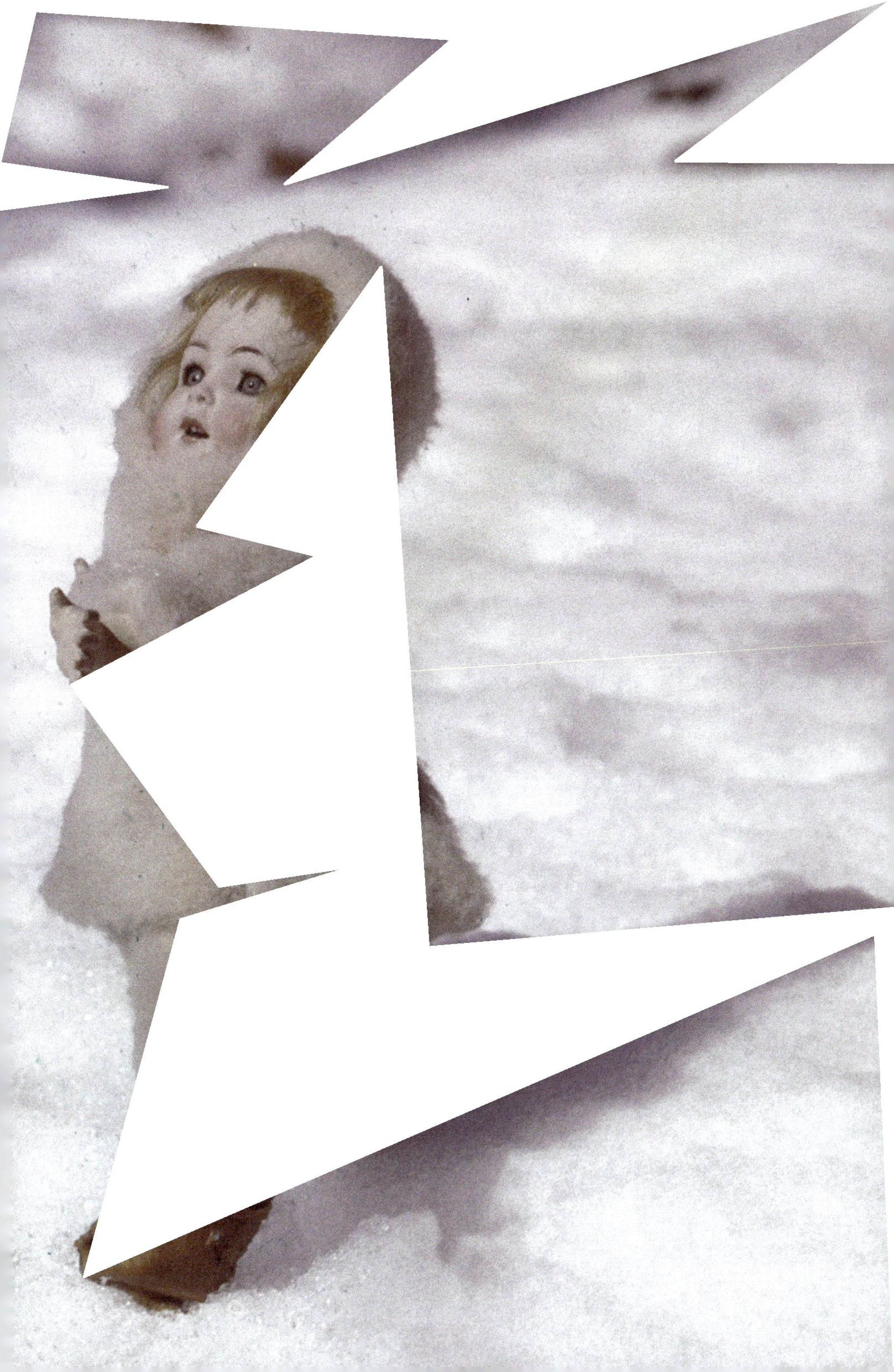

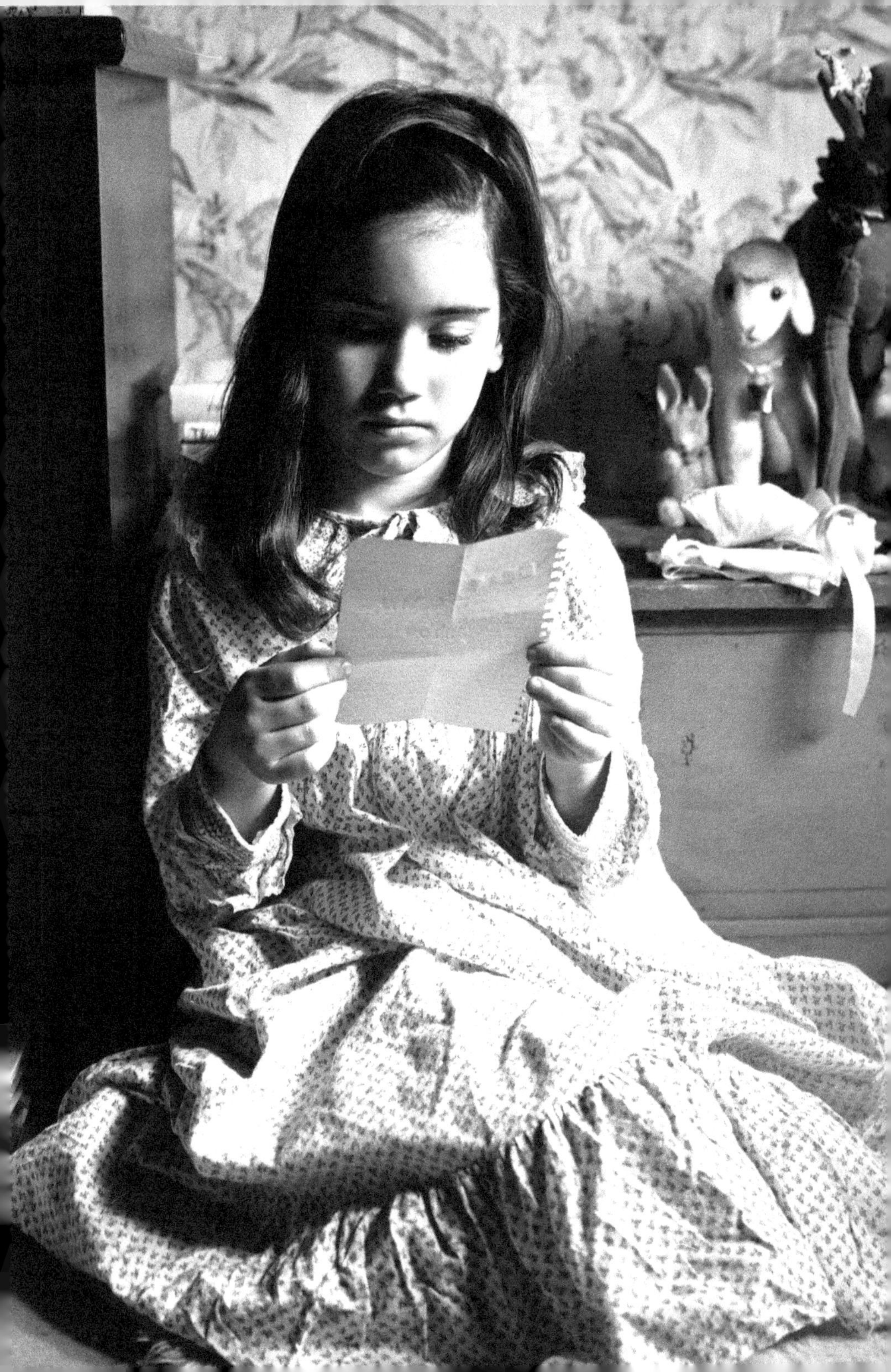

When Susan found the little pile of clothes and Robin's letter she didn't know what to think.

"She was only a doll. Dolls can't write letters. Dolls can't run away, can they?" wondered Susan, looking at her toys.

The toys only stared back in silence, but Robin and Sam were gone, and Susan never saw them again.

She thought of them, though.

When she was homesick for the country she thought, "This must have been the way that little doll felt when I took her away from the woods."

Never again was Susan quite sure just what a doll could or couldn't do.

Many a time she said to herself, "I wonder where that little doll is now? Wherever she is, I hope that she's happy."

Robin was!

She had her green woods, all her old friends, and Sam besides.

Crow grew quite fond of Sam in time, and scolded him as often as he scolded Robin.

Robin didn't care how much Crow scolded.

She didn't care how deep the snow fell in winter, nor how hot the sun shone in summer.

She didn't care if the woods dripped in the spring rains, or stood bare of leaves in the cold of autumn.

She slept as cozily under a leaf or two on the hard ground as though she were tucked up under a down quilt.

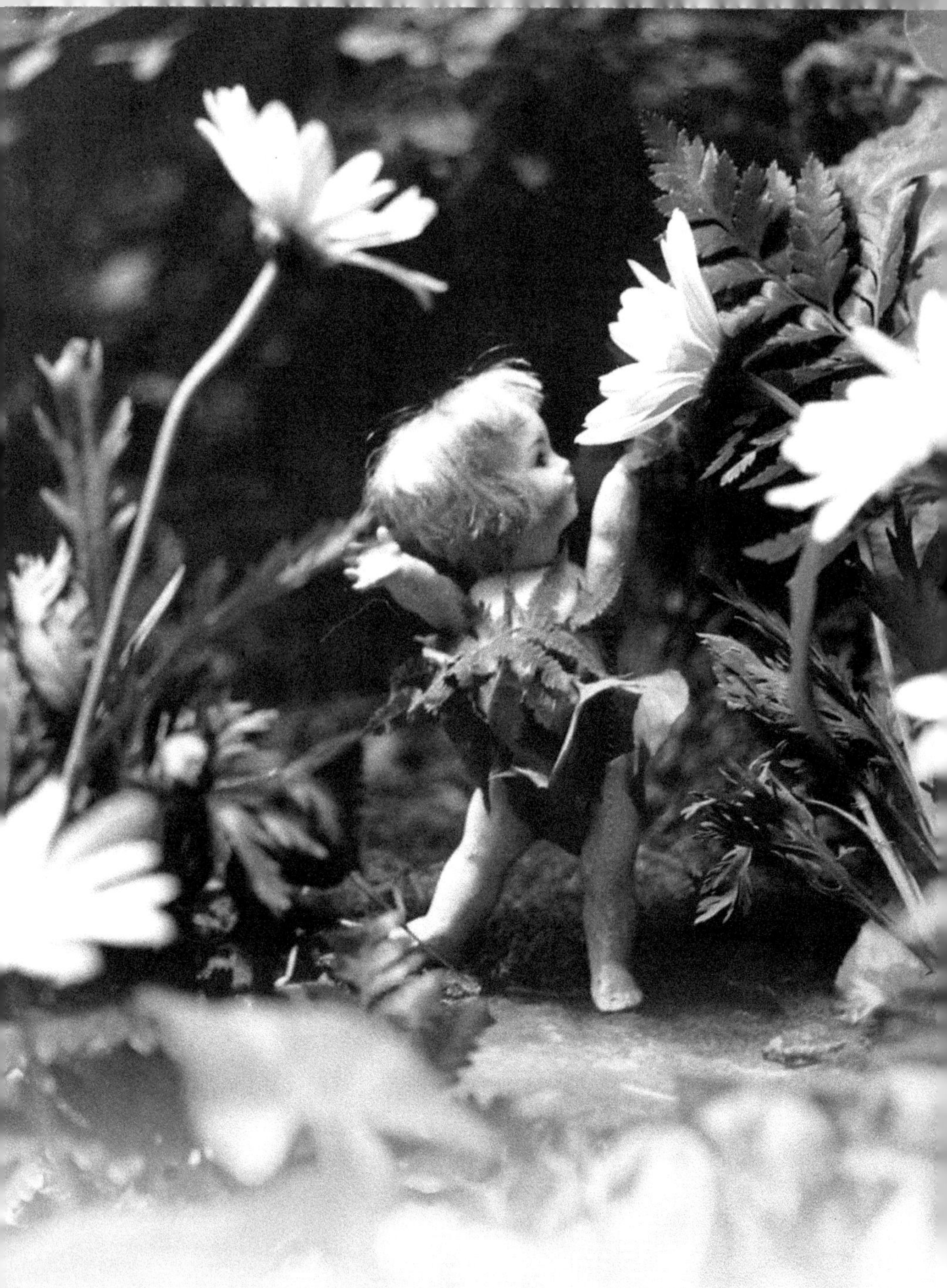

Oh, yes, Robin was happy.

Why wouldn't she be?

She was home!

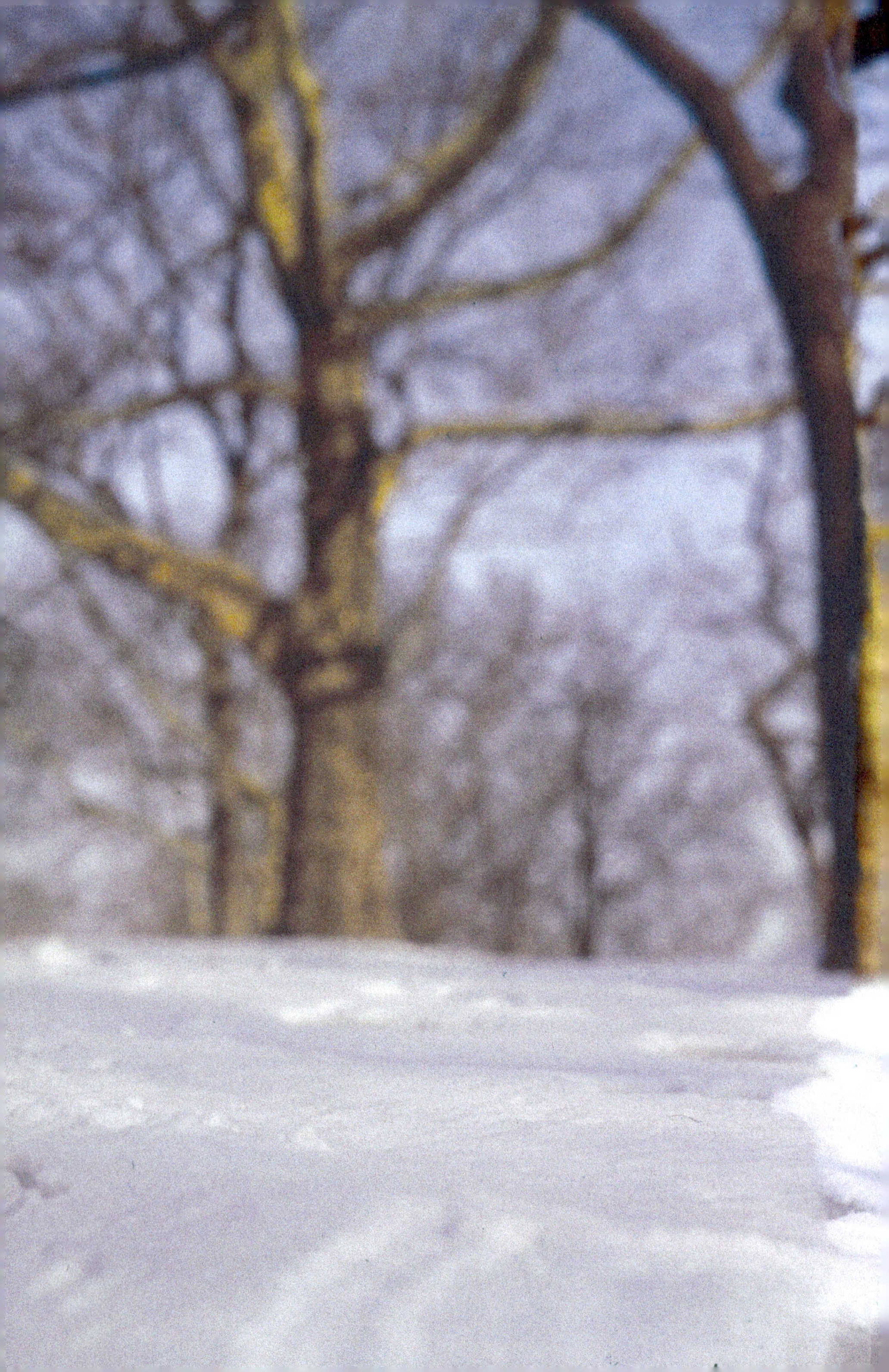

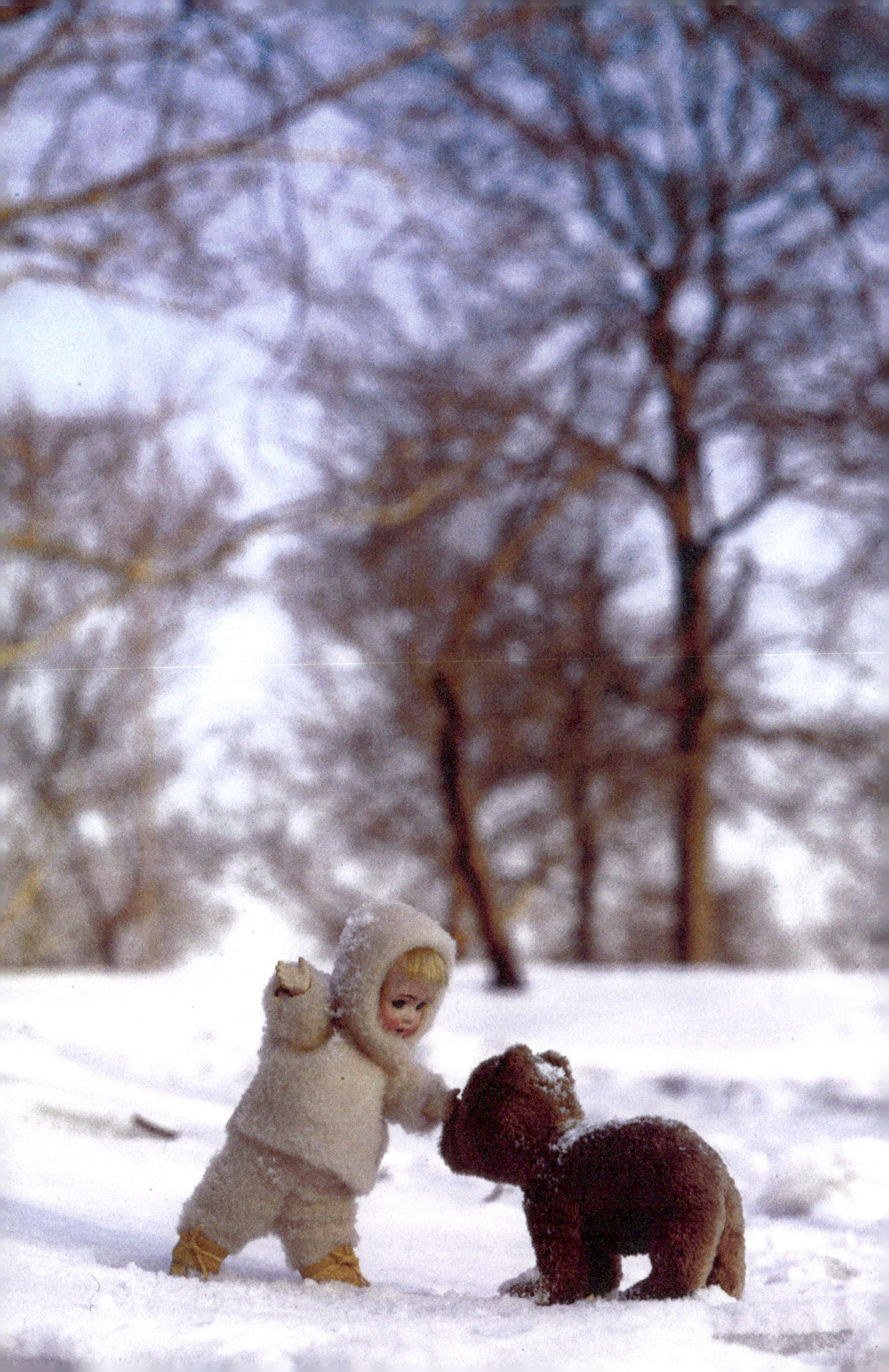

# DARE WRIGHT CHILDREN'S BOOKS IN PRINT

All are published by Dare Wright Media, LLC with the exception of *The Lonely Doll* which is published by Houghton Mifflin Harcourt.

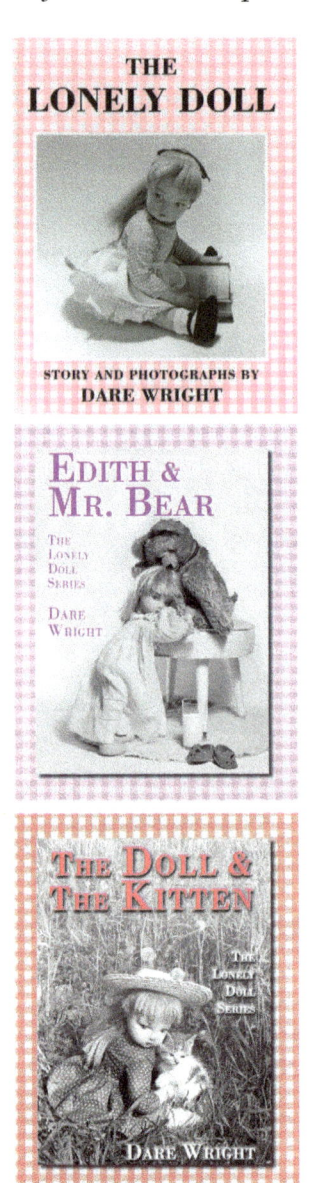

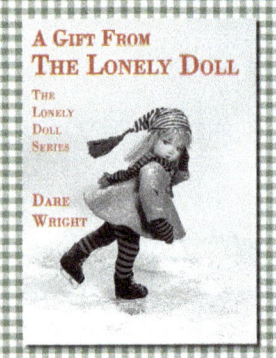

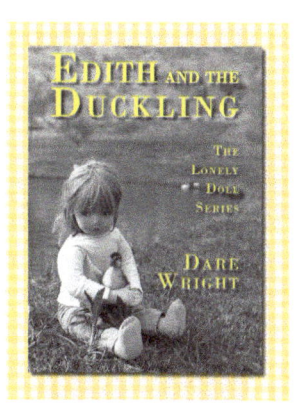

### Edith and the Duckling
The Lonely Doll Series
Dare Wright

### Edith & Little Bear Lend A Hand
The Lonely Doll Series
Dare Wright

### The Lonely Doll Learns A Lesson
The Lonely Doll Series
Dare Wright

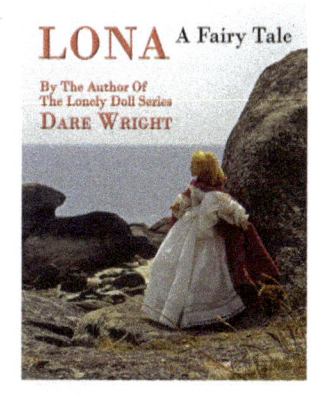

### Lona: A Fairy Tale
By The Author Of The Lonely Doll Series
Dare Wright

### Take Me Home
Story And Photographs By
Dare Wright
Author Of The Lonely Doll Series

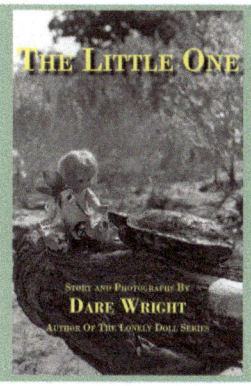

### The Little One
Story And Photographs By
Dare Wright
Author Of The Lonely Doll Series

### Make Me Real
Story And Photographs By
Dare Wright
Author Of The Lonely Doll Series

Milton Keynes UK
Ingram Content Group UK Ltd.
UKHW050017090524
442352UK00001BA/8